# Taking on the Title of *COACH*

*A 5 Step Guide for Coaching Youth Baseball and Softball*

By
Duke Baxter & Steve Nikorak
www.dominatethediamond.com

Copyright 2017

ISBN: 978-0-9789508-2-8

All rights reserved. Printed in the United States of America. No part of this publication may be reproduced or transmitted in any form or by any means without written permission of the author.

## This Book is dedicated to:

My Dad, Steve Nikorak Sr. whom I only got to spend 10 years of my life with before he passed away. He introduced me to the game of baseball and taught me the meaning of hard work. He taught me to be a good teammate, to be a leader and he taught me to believe in myself. He is pictured on the cover with me in 1995, my first year playing baseball.

Also to my Uncle Gary and Grandfather. Thank you for being my coaches in baseball and in life. Thank you for stepping in as father figures to my brothers and I and not only teaching us to be good players but good people. Forever grateful for everything you have done. - *Steve Nikorak*


I dedicate this book to all the amazing coaches that I have had the pleasure of playing under from little league, to high school, college, and pro ball. The lessons I was taught along the way has helped mold not only my baseball career but also my business, and my personal life. To this day I keep in touch with each of them because they weren't only my coaches, but now personal friends and mentors.

Also, to my dad whom even though he knew very little about sports (especially baseball) was always there to support me. He made it a point to always mention the good I did in a game. No matter what the score, results, or performance, he always said, "great game", and would pick out something good I did that day. Thanks, Dad for always being optimistic.

Mom, for the bumps and bruises you endured while playing catch with me in the backyard. Thank you, I love you. - ***Duke Baxter***

Special thanks to the following people for their commitment and assistance in making this book possible:

Christopher Kelly
Rose Marie Iskowitz

**ACKNOWLEDGEMENTS:**

Dan Hansen
Dom Lampasona
Matthew Baxter
Frankie Verano
Mikey Taylor

# Table of Contents

**Preface**................................................................i

**Chapter 1**
*Introduction & Impact of Being a Coach: Make Your Impact*.................................................... 1

**Chapter 2**
*Running the Perfect Practice* ........................... 4

**Chapter 3**
*Focus on Development* ................................. 47

**Chapter 4**
*In-Game Management* .................................. 54

**Chapter 5**
*Last Inning* ................................................... 60

# **Preface**

As former little league, high school, collegiate and professional baseball players, we appreciate the time, effort and dedication from every parent that takes on the role of coach. We know how challenging coaching can be and we want to do everything we can to help educate them.

Our vision was to create a step-by-step reference guide, for even the most inexperienced parents, to help them in every aspect of coaching. Our goal is to equip parents with all the tools necessary to become a first-time coach and get the absolute most out of their players. Building team chemistry, formulating drills and practice plans, keeping the game fun and communicating effectively with players are just a few of the qualities a coach must possess. This book will serve as a guide as you take on the title of coach.

We came up with the idea of writing a book a few years back after running one of our annual coach's clinics. Each year, we run free coach's clinics for neighboring Little Leagues, educating their coaches, most of whom are parents and have never coached before. In most cases, these parents have volunteered their time because their child asked them to coach their team. Without knowing what to do next, they attend our coach's clinic. After taking a 90-minute crash course in coaching, they realize they aren't nearly as prepared as they hoped they would be. They needed more information. They needed more drills. They needed help utilizing assistant coaches and volunteer parents. They needed help motivating their players. Most of all, they needed help keeping 12 kids engaged, all at once, in a sport where there tends to be a lot of standing around.

Each day, we're fortunate to coach and train kids of all ages and skill sets. We dedicate our lives to being good role models, mentors and leaders – on and off the field. We fully understand that as coaches, we have an obligation to lead by example because our impact can be life-changing. We're constantly trying to better ourselves and recognize that coaching is a never ending self-development process. Just like the players, we must strive to be better each day. We must educate ourselves and work hard to improve.

We've had the opportunity to play for some of the most renowned coaches in the game. We have also witnessed grown-ups act like children while managing little league teams. Our objective is to take all our experiences, the good and the bad and write this book. We want to give first time coaches the opportunity to use it as a reference point when entering their season. This will be the first book in our series on developing and mentoring young athletes and we're thrilled to see this vision come to fruition.

# **Chapter 1**
## *Introduction & Impact of Being a Coach: Make Your Impact*

Congratulations on taking on the title of COACH!

Whether you have experience coaching or you are beginning a new journey, there is always something new to learn and we cannot wait to get you started! Through this book, we will:

- Take you through every aspect of the game step by step and give you the tools necessary to make a positive impact on your players.
- Teach you how to develop each player and make the game fun for your team.

It is our job as coaches to encourage our children to keep playing the game we all grew up loving. A big part of this role is teaching them by modeling the life lessons learned through the game.

Baseball and softball are games of failure. They are self-esteem killers, they are difficult, and they will break your heart. These sports will make you laugh, cry, and celebrate all in one day.

We've all heard the cliché: "You get a hit three out of 10 times and you make the All-Star Team." *As* coaches, it's our job to teach our young players how to deal with failing the other seven times. Keeping our kids positive and optimistic will keep them playing these games even after it knocks them down.

We have a massive impact on every one of our players. It is our job to help them develop physically and mentally. How do we teach an eight-year-old to be resilient and continue to fight even when they're losing when we live in a world where our children can just press the reset button when they don't like how they're playing? This game will teach you to compete when you're down, to work hard, and most importantly, to respect your teammates, coaches, opposing teams, and umpires.

Softball and baseball are games where the participation numbers are dropping at the youth level. Our job as coaches is to stop that trend and make sure that baseball and softball are no longer the "boring" sports. In baseball, there are millions of Little Leaguers each year. That number drastically drops into the hundreds of thousands entering high school and even lower at the collegiate level. As youth coaches, we can slow down that decline and keep our kids playing the game as long as possible.

We want them to enjoy their experience and look back on it as a memorable one, not something that made them quit.

Legendary coach John Wooden once said, *"A good coach can change a game. A great coach can change a life."* We can all look back on our baseball careers and remember our favorite coaches. We can also remember growing up with the hopes and aspirations of playing in the big leagues. Assume your players know nothing about the game. Whether you're coaching baseball or softball, it's important to:

- Simplify the game.
- Use language they understand.
- Work with them individually to effectively develop their skills. Each player learns and develops differently. It is our job to find every one of our players' strengths and develop them accordingly.

Throughout this book, you will find different training methods, game plans, drill work, communication techniques, and practice plans to get the absolute most out of your players.

Always remember, this is a game and it is supposed to be fun. Our job as coaches is to lead by example and be positive role models for our young athletes. We're here to teach them to be good kids on the field and off. ***Good Luck!***

# Chapter 2
## *Running the Perfect Practice*

Running an efficient practice requires planning ahead on your part. Otherwise, it can be very easy for chaos to break out when you've got one coach running a practice with 12 kids who've never played the game before. Use the following blueprint to successfully plan and run your practice. Remember to keep it fun, organized, and informative.

## Part 1: There Must be Structure

Early in the season, it is essential to provide name tags to your players. Your coaching staff should also wear name tags so everybody on the team knows each other's name. Use first names only to keep it simple. The last thing you want is to be weeks into your season and have players whose names you still don't know or players who don't know their coaches' names. Nicknames are also a great way to interact with your players. Sometimes, it's easier to remember nicknames and using them can make it fun for your players to get to know each other.

On the very first day of practice, be sure to go over your rules and expectations for the team. Your demeanor on day one will set the tone for the entire season. When dealing with kids, you want to lay out your guidelines on day one and stick to them throughout the season.

Be sure to hold your players accountable. When they know there are consequences for their actions, they will learn from one another and you will earn their trust and respect. Explain the importance of having fun, but also paying attention to the rules and working hard.

Here are some sample rules and expectations to consider implementing with your team.

*<u>Tuck in your shirt.</u>* If you look sharp, you play sharp. Teach your players to look professional and take pride in wearing their jerseys correctly. Our players must respect the game and look the part!

Wearing your hat correctly is another example of wearing your uniform properly. Our young players who see big leaguers with their hats on backward tend to follow their lead, so it is your job to model and require they wear their uniform correctly. How the players on your team wear their uniforms is a direct reflection on the rest of the team's commitment to the sport.

> **"If you look sharp, you play sharp."**

*Hustle.* Hustling on and off the field is important from the very first practice through the duration of the player's career. The older you get, both in baseball and in life, the more important it becomes to hustle. Especially later in their careers, not hustling is a common reason why kids get cut from teams. Players instantly add more value to the team by out-working other players

*Always Take a Baseball Knee.* What's a baseball knee? A baseball knee is the position where players take a knee, not sitting down, with one foot on the ground.

Taking a baseball knee is important because it shows that players are ready to listen and take direction. At younger ages, players like to sit down and play with the dirt/grass. When your players are not in a baseball knee position, it is very easy for them to lose focus and miss out on your instructions for the day.

*Respect Your Teammates.* As coaches, we might assume that our players know how to respect their teammates and opponents. But don't assume anything. In many cases, we must teach our players to be good *team* players. Too often, kids get picked on for failing or making a mistake. It is our job as coaches to make sure we teach the importance of picking each other up and playing together with respect for everyone on the team as well as our opponents.

*Respect the Game.* What does it mean to respect the game? Respecting the game means to respect your teammates, the opposing teams, all coaches, and the umpires. When we teach our players to respect their teammates, it means to cheer them on, pick them up when they're down, and support them when they are successful.

To respect the opposing team means to cheer for your own teammates without disrespecting the other team. It means that after every game, regardless of the result, our players are to give high fives and say "good game" to each player on the other team.

Respecting the umpire means to shake his/her hand after the game and say "thank you." Too often, we lose sight of the fact that an umpire's job is a difficult one. In most cases they are volunteering, taking time from their life to help out the league.

> **"Respecting the game means to respect your teammates, opposing teams, coaches and umpires."**

One excellent concept to implement is the *Word of the Day*. Each day, provide your team with a new Word of the Day to focus on during practice. Examples of this might be *Hustle, Compete, Communication, Focus,* and *Teamwork.*

Ask your players at the start of practice what they think the word means. Once you get their feedback, explain your definition, why it's important, and how it pertains to the game. You can touch on this word throughout practice and throughout the different drills and skills. By doing this, you're teaching your kids both the mechanics of the game as well as the character traits they will take with them off the field.

Each day when you start practice, get down on a knee with your team. We want to communicate *with* them, not talk down to them. They will respond much better and retain better eye contact through your pre-practice talk if you are speaking at their level. Go over your game plan and explain the importance of making eye contact with the coach when the coach is speaking. Communicate with them, ask them questions, include them in the discussion, and make them speak up.

At this point, you can go over your practice plan for the day. It is essential to have a practice plan each day and post it for your team. This adds organization to your practice and gives the players ownership of what is going to happen.

It is very easy as a coach to get repetitive and do the same drills all the time. This is where practice gets boring for your team. Including a variety of drills in your practice plan will help with keeping their attention and developing their skills.

It is also very easy to forget some of the key points you initially wanted to cover once you get halfway through practice. There are multiple ways to teach each skill set and by changing the stations each practice, you will keep your players engaged and focused. Save your practice plans so you can look back on a week-to-week basis to make adjustments.

## Sample Practice Plan

| | Team Name: Zoned Elite<br>Location: 24 Kearney St. Bridgewater NJ | | Date: 1-1-17<br>Time: 5:30 – 7:00 |
|---|---|---|---|
| **TIME** | **ACTIVITY** | **COACHES** | **LOCATION** |
| 5:30 – 5:35 | Introduction – Rules - Expectations | Coach Steve | Left Field Line |
| 5:35 – 5:45 | Dynamic Warm-Up<br>Throwing Program | Coach Steve<br>Coach Duke<br>Coach Chris | Left Field Line |
| 5:45 – 5:50 | Introduction of Signs | Coach Duke | 3rd Base Area |
| 5:50 – 6:00 | Base Running<br>1. Home to 1st<br>2. 1st to 3rd | Coach Steve<br>Coach Duke<br>Coach Chris | Infield Area |
| 6:00 – 6:30 | Break into 3 Stations (10 Min each)<br>1. Groundballs<br>2. Fly Balls<br>3. Hitting – Batting Practice | Coach Duke<br>Coach Steve<br>Coach Chris | Short Stop<br>Center Field<br>Batting Cages |
| 6:30 – 6:50 | Situational Defense:<br>1. Force vs. Tag Plays<br>2. Bunt Defense | Coach Steve<br>Coach Duke<br>Coach Chris | Full Field |
| 6:50 – 7:00 | Team Building Activity:<br>1. Relay Race – Set up cones and divide the teams into 2 groups randomly.<br>*Great way to do conditioning in a fun way where you can teach your players to pick each other up and cheer one another on | Coach Steve<br>Coach Duke<br>Coach Chris | Right Field<br>*Start at Foul line and sprint out and around the cone & back.* |

Incorporate a dynamic warm-up directly after your introduction. Using cones, put your players into lines and structure a warm-up to follow at the start of every practice. Keep the warm-up the same each week. Walk your players through the warm-up and after a few weeks, assign one of the leaders on your team to run the dynamic warm-up on their own. Explain the importance of looking uniform and getting the blood flowing and a good sweat at the start of each practice. Aside from safety and activating your muscles, a structured warm-up will add discipline, assign leadership, and prepare your team for an organized practice each week. Below is an example of a dynamic warm-up:

1. 50% jog – 60 ft.
2. High Knees for 30 ft. followed by light jog
3. Butt Kicks for 30 ft. followed by a light jog
4. Side Shuffles – 60 ft.
5. Karaoke – 60 ft.
6. Lunge with a twist – 60 ft.
7. Back Pedal – 60 ft.
8. Two Shuffles & Sprint – 60 ft.

Directly after the dynamic warm-up is a perfect time to go over base running, secondary leads, and steal breaks. During each practice, it is important to touch on some aspect of base running. Explain the importance of hustling down the base path the same speed regardless of how well you hit the baseball. Teach the difference between running *through* first base on a ground ball to the infield and taking a *hard turn* around first base on a base hit to the outfield. On a ground ball to the infield, we want to accelerate through first base, in a straight line, without slowing down. On a base hit, we want to make a hard turn anticipating that the outfielder makes an error so we can go on to second base.

On all baseball fields, secondary leads are very important. On 46/60 ft. baseball fields, there is no leading. Once you get to the 50/70 ft. diamond, your team can lead. In both scenarios, you must teach your players to shuffle off the base in an athletic position to be ready for the next play to happen. On 46/60 ft. fields, when the baseball is crossing home plate, you want your players to take a shuffle off the base. On 50/70 ft. fields, when the pitcher begins their delivery to home plate, you want your players to take 2 shuffles toward the next base, timing it so their feet hit the ground as the ball is entering the hitting zone. This will put your players in an athletic position and will allow for much faster reactions to the play developing.

Pictured below is the correct position on 46/60 fields where leading is not allowed:

If you're coaching players on the 50/70 or 60/90 field, you must go over a primary lead. This is the initial lead they take off the base while the pitcher is getting ready to throw to home plate. The simplest way to teach it is for the player to start with their heels on the base while they get the sign from the 3$^{rd}$ base coach. After receiving the sign, once the pitcher is on the rubber, they can take a step off the base with their left foot, then turn toward home plate while stepping with the right and proceed to shuffle the correct distance off the base. The ideal distance off the base would be one step and one dive back to the base to determine if they are far enough off without getting picked off.

Pictured below is the correct position for a primary lead:

Depending on your team's ability level, a throwing program is an important part of any practice. You don't want to look at your team and tell them, "Go get loose down the left field line." Have your players start out on a knee and progressively move back together. A good way to organize it is to time the throwing program. It is not a good idea to have your team play catch right away if you're coaching tee ball or younger players.

If they're just starting out, make throwing and catching separate stations in practice to avoid injury.

If your team can play catch safely, express the importance of playing catch with a purpose. A lot of young players will just play catch to get loose. We, as coaches, want to force our players to play catch to get better. If we cannot control the baseball in warm-ups, how do we expect to control the ball in live game situations? Put pressure on them. After every dropped baseball, make them sprint across and switch sides with their throwing partner. This will force them to focus a little more and you will begin to see your team play catch a lot better before practice and games.

Below is an example of a basic throwing program.

1. Light toss on one knee (15 ft.) *(1 Minute)*
   From 15 feet away, have each player put an arm up in front of their body (shown below) in the shape of an "L". Have them snap the ball back and forth, focusing on snapping their wrist and emphasizing four-seam rotation on the baseball.

2. Rotational throwing (30 ft.) *(1 Minute)*

From 30 feet away, have your players line up with their feet (10 toes) facing their throwing partner. The idea here is to not use their lower body at all. We want to rotate from the hips up and focus on extension and reaching out toward their partners.

3. Short Toss (45 ft.) *(1 Minute)*

From roughly 45 feet away, have your players line up with their glove side facing their throwing partners and begin to play catch. The idea here is to transfer the weight from the back leg to the front leg while extending out and hitting their partner in the chest.

4. Shuffle and Throw (50 – 60 ft.) *(2 Minutes)*

Just like short toss, but from 50-60 feet away, have your players shuffle into their throw. This is essential when we move back to longer distances. It will allow your players to be athletic and incorporate some momentum into their throws.

5. Long Toss (On a line – or One Long Hop) *(1 Minute)*

Long toss is extremely important when we talk about building arm strength. We want our players to go back as far as they can while still having the strength to reach their partners without having too much arc in their throws. If they are unable to reach, it is okay for a player to give their partner a long hop. You should only have your players long toss for about a minute.

6. Shorten back up and work on quick transfers *(30 seconds)*

Working on quick transfers is a great drill that relates to many in-game situations. You can put pressure on your players and force them to work on catching and throwing the ball at a fast pace while turning their feet and shoulders to line them up with their partners.

## Part 2: Use Stations

To keep your team engaged and focused, create stations and keep them moving. We've all seen this situation before when a team tries to do "infield/outfield practice":

> **Coach:** *Hits a fly ball way over the left fielder's head.*
> **Left Fielder:** *Runs, picks it up, and heaves it in over the cutoff man's head.*
> **Shortstop:** *Picks up the ball and throws it to second base.*
> **Second Baseman:** *Drops the ball, picks it up, and throws it over the catcher.*
> **Catcher:** *Picks the ball up and hands it back to the coach.*
> **Coach:** *Repeats the same thing with the center fielder.*

By the time the first baseman even touches the baseball, you're already 10 minutes into practice and now the game becomes "boring." Remember, we want to keep our players active and engaged during practice. The best way to maximize your practice time is to set up short stations, each focusing on a different skill set.

Below is an example of what the field might look like with four stations set up, utilizing the entire field:

A 5 Step Guide for Teaching Youth Baseball and Softball

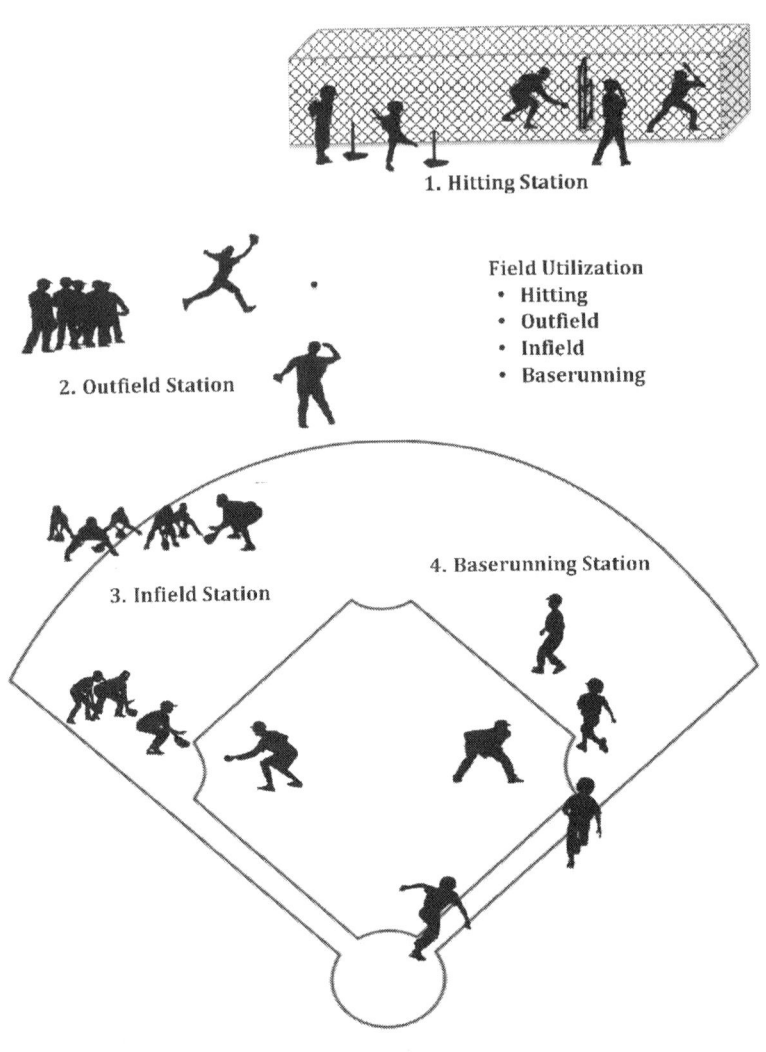

You want to utilize your assistant coaches and any parents that want to volunteer and help. If you set up four 10-minute stations, practice will move a lot quicker, your players will get more reps, and they will be more engaged while practicing each skill. Set up your stations ahead of time and go over your practice plans with your assistant coaches/parents to ensure a smooth, productive practice.

After teaching the basics of each station, it is best to create game-like situations for your players to work through. We want our players to communicate with one another. We want to put pressure on them in practice so that it is less difficult when they play in a game – their high level of preparation will make the real game feel "easy" and more fun. Especially when working with younger kids, we want to create fun competitions out of everything. Give out small prizes like bubble gum to the winners and watch how much harder they work and how much their focus increases.

## Below are just a few examples of competitions you can use:

*Target Practice:* Instead of having your young players play catch, set up a target for them to aim for. This could be a tee with a softball on it, a sign attached to a fence, or any other target you can create. Create a points system and have fun with the players. If possible, use the fence or a batting cage to keep the balls contained to a small area, making it quicker and easier to pick up when practice is over.

*Batting Practice:* Rather than just taking batting practice, play "W*iffle Ball Home Run Derby.*" Set up cones or lines with a points system and allow your players to swing free, fearlessly, and aggressively. We want our players to want to swing. We don't want them to be afraid to fail. We can all remember being kids and "swinging for the fences" when we played Wiffle ball outside with our friends. This is the perfect drill to let them have fun, swing hard, and compete with their friends at practice. Below is a picture of what the station might look like.

*Touchdown Drill:* When teaching your players to catch fly balls, have them start on a line and run out like they would as a wide receiver in football. This will teach them to hustle after fly balls and you can make it a competition among the players.

At the end of each practice, it is best to have a team-building exercise and/or competition. Put some pressure on your players and make them work together and cheer each other on. This will help them learn to work together as a team and create positive energy among themselves. You could create a relay race, a throwing competition, or even coach pitch scrimmage to make it as game-like as possible. Talk them through the activity and teach them how to cheer on their teammates through high fives, positive words, and phrases like "You can do it!" or "Way to go, good try, keep going!"

> **Teach them how to work together as a team and create positive energy.**

# Part 3: Utilizing Small and/or Indoor Areas

As mentioned earlier, it is extremely difficult to get your players a lot of reps and develop their skills on a big field with just one coach hitting fly balls from home plate. Try to do all our drill work in controlled environments. Once you break your team into stations, focus on one skill with four or five kids and you will see much more improvement and concentration from your players.

## Shrink the Field

Whether you're working on ground balls, pop ups, communication, or throwing, it is much easier to do it in one small area of the field.

*Ground Balls:* Put your kids in a line and go over the proper fielding position. After that, you can roll ground balls to them at a fast pace. This will allow you to break down each individual and get them plenty of reps. It also builds confidence and will allow you to make the transition to hitting them ground balls a lot faster.

*Pop Ups:* You can teach a small group of kids the proper mechanics of catching a pop up, then start gradually tossing the balls up in the air. You can progress to tossing them higher and even have them communicate to one another saying, "I got it!" or "Mine!"

*Throwing:* Have your players line up and throw balls at a target. You can break down each player's mechanics this way, and they will get a lot more out of it than just doing a warm-up playing catch together. Don't forget to make it a competition.

Your players should stand in an athletic position with the back of their glove facing their target when they begin to throw. Their arms should be relaxed with some flex in them and they should be looking at their target. The ball should be out of the glove and facing almost all the way behind them.

*Catching the Ball:* At the younger ages, this is one of the more difficult skills to teach. Most kids don't know how to position their glove correctly or they try to get out of the way every time the ball is thrown to them. Using tennis balls or squishy balls, teach your players how to catch the ball with their fingers up. Most kids will flip their glove upside down to try to get out of the way, but that actually puts them at a higher risk of injury. After they can catch the ball with confidence, you can have them back up, then throw the ball overhand to them.

> "Using tennis balls or squishy balls, teach your players how to catch the ball with their fingers up!"

Pictured below is the "Windshield Wiper Drill." This is a simple drill that teaches your kids to keep their fingers up even when the ball is thrown to their arm side. Using the squishy balls, have your players move their arms across their bodies like windshield wipers to catch or smack the balls with their fingers pointing upward.

*Hitting:* Start out with basic hitting mechanics for your younger players. Focus on their balance, timing, and being aggressive. Too often, we fill our younger players' heads with too much terminology. Simplify the game to create confident hitters!

Set up stations for your players to work on their swings. Tees, a side toss station, and a front toss station are three basic stations where your players can get a lot of repetitions. Don't go straight to overhand batting practice. You will find that your tosses are a lot more accurate and controlled. Slowly building up to overhand pitches will allow for your players' gradual batting development, which will lead to a confident, aggressive swing.

When teaching hitting to younger players, it is important to simplify the process. Use the following guidelines to help yourself and your players understand the swing easily.

**Step 1 – Stance**: It is important to start in a comfortable, balanced position. Feet should be slightly wider than shoulder width apart. The hitter should be relaxed, with their hands raised slightly off their back shoulder.

**Step 2 - The Load**: The load is crucial for any hitter to be on time and in rhythm with the pitcher. As you can see in the picture below, the batter's hands are working back toward the catcher, almost as if they are winding up to throw a punch. At the same time, the hitter is taking a small step toward the pitcher. This creates momentum and puts them in a strong, athletic, and balanced position to hit. Remember, timing is everything! There should be rhythm and the swing should be smooth!

**Step 3 – Connection**: The lower half will trigger the start of the swing. As you can see, the back knee is starting to drive toward the front foot, creating tension in the core. The hands begin to work toward the baseball and the batter's back elbow is connected to the hip. This creates the shortest, strongest bat path to contact.

**Step 4 – Contact**: At contact, it is important to make sure your players are balanced and their weight is still centered in the middle of their bodies. The back elbow is still tight against the body and they must focus on accelerating through the ball.

**Step 5 – Extension**: As you can see, the player has already hit the ball and their bat is continuing to move toward the pitcher. Most young players will hit the ball and immediately roll their hands across their front hip. Getting to extension is important for power and keeping your bat in the hitting zone for a long time.

**Step 6 – Finish**: Even though the ball has already left the bat, we must teach our players to stay balanced throughout the entire swing. Most young players struggle to stay balanced the whole time. Failing to teach good posture and balance at an early age will create bad habits. Poor balance will break down their mechanics and create inconsistency.

## Part 4: Use Props

It only takes one incidence of getting hit in the face with a ball to ruin a young player's confidence. If you are coaching first-time players, we strongly suggest using Wiffle balls, Incrediballs, and squishy balls for all skill sets. As mentioned earlier, this will allow your players to start to play with confidence, which will make it easier to teach them the proper mechanics of each skill set. Each week, you can move onto harder drills and more realistic game speed movements. Before you know it, they will be using real baseballs and ready to compete in game situations.

For hitting, younger players can struggle with making contact with the baseball or softball. This can be discouraging. A lot of players at the tee ball age haven't yet developed good hand-eye coordination, so a good idea is to start out letting them hit dodgeballs. They will consistently make contact, which will make hitting stations a lot more fun for your players. You can use the dodgeballs both on the tee as well as in soft toss. As you see the players progress, challenge them with smaller balls to keep developing their skill sets.

When teaching your players to field ground balls for the first time, we also suggest using paddles or Hot Hands Extreme. This will force them to use two hands, allowing for the correct fielding technique, a faster transition, and safer positioning for your young players. Pictured below are a few of the drills you can do with props as coaches:

*Paddle Drill:* Line your players up and roll ground balls to them using the paddles to emphasize using two hands and making quick transfers.

*Hot Hands Extreme Drill:* Line your players up and roll ground balls to them or toss them fly balls. Emphasize using two hands and when they separate to throw the ball, the Hot Hands will break apart, allowing the players to complete their throws.

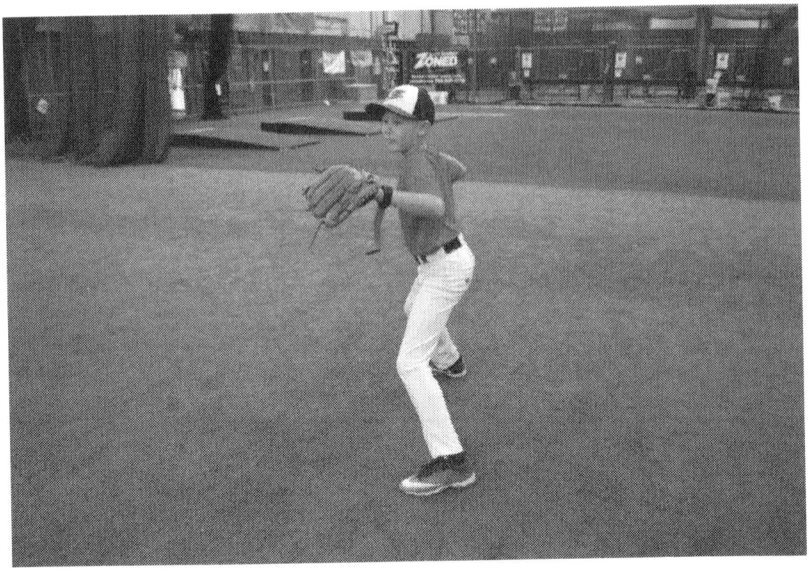
ZONED

# Chapter 3
## *Focus on Development*

It is crucial for coaches to focus on their players' development over their teams' records. The wins and losses don't matter at young ages and too often, coaches put too much added pressure on kids because of how bad *they* want to win. This game isn't about the coaches, it's about the players. It's about making the sport fun and enjoyable for everyone on the team. As former big leaguer Mike Matheny said, *"Sports should be about kids and their passion, not about parents and their goals."*

We want to create a competitiveness within our players that they can take with them through life. This competitiveness will bring them wins, but it is just as important to experience and learn from losses. We cannot lose sight of the fact that the game of baseball/softball is a never-ending development process. Our kids will never master their respective games, but they can work hard to be the best athletes they can be.

> **"We cannot lose sight of the fact that the game of baseball/softball is a never-ending development process."**

As coaches, it is our job to build a strong foundation for our players that will help them for the rest of their careers. As mentioned earlier, the Word of the Day is a great start. These character traits, such as sportsmanship, hard work, and dedication are qualities they will carry with them in school, sports, and life. You will leave a tremendous impression on your players. They will look up to you and follow your actions, good or bad.

We as coaches, need to teach our players to play with a short memory. We can learn from our mistakes and move forward. Whether you're 0-3 with three strike outs or 3-3 with three doubles, the fourth at bat is just as important. This can be one of the more difficult things to teach as a coach. Often, your players will get frustrated, upset, and let their emotions dictate their performance for the rest of the game. Use phrases like "So what?" and "Flush it" to teach your players to move onto the next play and stay focused on playing well.

We need to teach them to carry themselves with confidence and show good body language. Body language is contagious. When you have one player hang his head and pout, you will begin to see other players on the team act the same way. Your players feed off one another. Let your players know that the fans shouldn't be able to tell whether they're winning, losing, or tied going into the last inning; the body language should be the same in all situations.

It is our job as coaches to help develop team-oriented players. Too many parents and players focus on "What's next?" "What level is after this?" "What is the next step?" We need to teach our players to focus on staying in the moment and playing for their teams. Too often, our players get caught up focusing on their future careers instead of enjoying the journey and the teams they currently play for. We want our players to put the team before their own individual accomplishments. When coaches can create a culture focused on group accomplishments and teamwork, we begin to see true development take place.

As you get older, no one will remember your batting average at 10U. We need to make sure that we don't put too much emphasis on statistics. One statistic that we do keep is quality at-bats. (QAB). If one of our players goes up to the plate and hits a line drive to the center fielder, the book says 0-1, but we count it as a quality at-bat. Some characteristics of a QAB might be:

- A hard hit.
- An aggressive swing.
- Moving a runner over.
- Getting a bunt down.
- Battling at the plate.

You can reward your players by giving out stickers at the end of the week for each QAB they had during their games. This will motivate your players, especially that ones that don't usually hit a high average. You'll begin to see your players focus on battling and competing in each at bat they have.

When we speak to our players, we must simplify the game. We cannot use big words or try to make our players swing like the major leaguers we see on TV. This is unrealistic and unfair to our kids. Even the best players in the world try to simplify the game. It is always good to take a step back and put yourself in the player's shoes. If you were 10 years old, would you understand the directions you're giving?

> **If our players go up to the plate and hit a line drive to the center fielder, the book says 0-1, but we count it as a *Quality at Bat. (QAB)***

**Athletes learn three different ways:** *Seeing, Hearing* **and** *Feeling*

**Seeing:** It is important that as coaches, we can demonstrate the techniques and mechanics of the skills we teach in an easy way. Video always works, as does the coach physically demonstrating the skills front of the player or team.

Visual learners use pictures, videos, and diagrams to best understand certain skills or techniques. We must be able to pick up a bat or glove and show our players the correct way to use it.

We don't want to tell them what to do without having the ability to perform the swing or technique.

**Hearing:** Auditory learners prefer to listen to a coach explain how or why we do certain things on the field, as opposed to seeing it. It is important to communicate with our players in simple terms. We need to relate to them, build confidence within them, and provide positive feedback.

You will learn right away which players need to be pushed and which players need you to coddle them. Certain players love high-pressure situations and others panic and get nervous. It is our job to prepare our players and condition them ahead of time to play with poise. This comes from continuous positive reinforcement and a whole lot of practice.

**Feeling:** As coaches, we need to walk our players through the mechanics of every skill. Kinesthetic learners prefer to learn by carrying out the activity or skill on the field. We need to let them feel what they need to do to create muscle memory. If we don't teach them correctly and they do it wrong, it is our fault.

Creating checkpoints for them to follow or using terms they can understand will increase your chance of getting them to repeat the same skill. Having your players perform the technique in slow motion is also a great way to get them to remember the feeling.

# Chapter 4
## *In-Game Management*

Practice time is for **coaches and instruction.** Game time is for the kids! We don't want to find ourselves over-coaching our players during games. Games are for the players to compete and have fun. We don't want to fill their heads with mechanical thoughts during games but rather, pump them with confidence. We've all seen the coaches coaching 3rd base, telling the hitter to do something mechanical, then the kid steps in the batter's box and their parents are sitting behind the backstop, telling them something different. How is the kid supposed to compete against the pitcher with so many thoughts going on in their head?

Take a step back and let them play. During a game, try to put yourself in the kid's shoes. One concept we like to use is help them make athletic adjustments instead of creating mechanical thoughts. If your players are struggling to do something in the game, give them something athletic to think about.

An example of this might be:
**Player:** Right-handed batter struggling with timing. They continue to roll over the ball because they are way out in front and swinging too early.

**Coach:** Instead of saying something like:

- "Keep your hands back"
- "Wait longer & Don't Drift!"
- "Stay inside the ball"
- Say something in between innings like: "Try to crush a line drive at the second baseman" "Hit the ball as hard as you can at the right fielder!"

In this instance, your player will be going up to the plate with a confident approach and game plan. They are no longer thinking about the mechanics of doing something and instead, they are competing with a goal in mind.

It is extremely important that you have a game plan going into the game. It is best to set your line-up and defensive assignments ahead of time so when you get to the field, all your focus can be on your players. When you get to the field, you want to be out communicating with your team when they're warming up, not sitting in the dugout writing out your line-up. You don't want to be in the dugout with all 12 players yelling at you, asking, *"Where am I playing next inning?"*

> "It is extremely important that we have a game plan going into the game. It is best to set your line-up and defensive assignments ahead of time so when you get to the field all your focus can be on your players."

Prepare everything before you get to the field so you can post it in the dugout and your players know where they're going each inning. This will allow you to manage all 12 players and give them each an opportunity for fair playing time. You can always make adjustments to the line-up card during the game, but it is essential to have a blueprint. Here is an example line-up card detailing out the positions of the players for the full game.

| REDHAWKS | 1 | 2 | 3 | 4 | 5 | 6 | 7 |
|---|---|---|---|---|---|---|---|
| 1. | | | | | | | |
| 2. | | | | | | | |
| 3. | | | | | | | |
| 4. | | | | | | | |
| 5. | | | | | | | |
| 6. | | | | | | | |
| 7. | | | | | | | |
| 8. | | | | | | | |
| 9. | | | | | | | |
| 10. | | | | | | | |
| 11. | | | | | | | |
| 12. | | | | | | | |
| 13. | | | | | | | |

Date: _____ Coaches: _____
Opponent: _____ Location: _____

As coaches, we want to make everything a learning experience. You should always keep notes throughout the game, writing down both positives and negatives that occur. Kids and parents always remember the "big moment." Our job is to document the small moments and emphasize the importance of doing all the little things correctly throughout the game that might effect that big moment. At the end of the game, you should mention some of the situations that occurred during the game that helped your team succeed or fail. With losses, it can be very difficult to look back and remember anything positive that happened. We should always leave our players with a positive note after a big loss. Touch on some of the things they did well and allow them to learn and grow from their mistakes. Allow them to leave the field with smiles on their faces and the intent to work hard before the next game.

Always remember, when dealing with player-parent issues, you are talking about someone's *child*. Regardless of the situation, parents will come to the defense of their children and it is important that we as coaches don't lose sight of that. Don't take it personal if you end up on the bad end of a complaint from a parent in the heat of the moment. Whether it is playing time concerns or general issues about the team, it is a good idea to create a 24 hour policy for your parents when they have a complaint they want to discuss. In most cases, they will calm down and approach you in a different fashion then they would after a game. Take a step back, take a deep breath and always respect the parent's emotions.

As we've mentioned many times, we need to fill our kids' heads with confidence. Regardless of numbers, statistics, or wins and losses, we want our players to not be afraid to fail. Too often, players are worried about letting down their teammates, parents and coaches. Preach the importance of quality at-bats, throwing strikes, being the first one on and off the field, outworking the other team, and staying positive. Failure is going to happen. It is inevitable and will happen every time they step onto the diamond.

Preparation is the key to managing and learning from these failures. Knowing ahead of time that they're going to make errors and strike out at times can ease the embarrassment of it happening in a big situation.

# Chapter 5
## *Last Inning*

Your impact on your players can change their lives. You can play a key role in shaping the future of someone's baseball or softball career. You also have the ability make their experience an unhappy one and be the reason why they quit the game. Never forget that in a game where we fail so often, it is crucial to provide positive reinforcement. We must teach our players to believe in themselves and to play as a team. We must be organized, have a game plan, and be prepared to be both a coach and role model.

> "We need to fill our kids heads with confidence! Regardless of numbers, statistics, or wins and losses... we want our players Not Afraid to Fail!"

This game isn't about us and it isn't about our career "back in the day." It is about the development of our youth and providing them with a strong foundation of character and work ethic. The players on your team will look up to you for guidance and they will follow your actions. It is not uncommon to see coaches say one thing, but their body language says something totally different. Players often look to us for our approval. Even though we might think we are being positive, if we give off negative body language, it is going to send a contradicting message. And when there is a contradicting message, people go with the visual – they go with what they see.

We must respect the game, respect opposing teams, and umpires. We need to teach them how to play the game hard, to be good teammates and good people both on and off the field.

The life lessons this game offers are endless. It will give your players the opportunity to meet lifelong friends, teach them discipline, and show them how to battle through adversity. Never forget that your players see everything. Be a leader for them. Have fun and develop their skills with them. Pick them up when they are down, discipline them when they aren't working hard, and lay the groundwork for the rest of their career.

> "Players see everything. They look up to you. Be a leader for them. Have FUN and develop them! Pick them up when they are down, discipline them when they aren't working hard and lay the groundwork for the rest of their career!"

*Good luck and be the best coach you can be!*

As a small token of our appreciation for purchasing this book, use coupon code:
**DTDBOOK414**
at checkout to receive a discount on our **online video training course** for **Rookies, Minors & Majors**.

**www.DominateTheDiamond.com**

Made in the USA
Columbia, SC
03 September 2017